Into the

poems

by Sarah James

Circaidy Gregory Press

Into the Yell

Poems by Sarah James
Copyright Information

Printed in the UK by the
MPG Books Group Bodmin & King's Lynn

ISBN 978-1-906451-24-0

Published by Circaidy Gregory Press
Creative Media Centre, 45 Robertson St, Hastings,
Sussex TN34 1HL

www.circaidygregory.co.uk
Independent Books for Independent Readers

Circaidy Gregory Press would like to thank the artists...

Julie Haller was born in Worcestershire in 1975 and her first post-school qualification was a BTEC National Diploma in Art and Design. This then led her on to 3D Design in Ceramics at Wolverhampton University, where she graduated in 1998 with a BA (Hons). Her artistic background also includes three years' experience as part of a Marks and Spencer window dressing team. Julie's current work ranges from photography and illustrations to detailed room designs, murals and fine art painting. Her art also features on the publicity posters for *Into the Yell*.

Sam Hutchcocks was born in Edgbaston, Birmingham, in 1967. In her early college years, Sam gained ONC and HND in Technical Illustration at Bournville College of Art. Following this, she attended Wolverhampton University and successfully obtained a B.Ed (Hons), with Art as the main subject. Her past work includes portrait commissions, mural paintings and setting up and running her own art group.

Artistically, Sam and Julie have been collaborating for four years. Through their Worcestershire-based business, Moonlit Murals, they create children's murals, trompe l'oeil room features, book covers and poster designs. All commissions considered, they can be contacted via the email address below.

moonlitmurals@ymail.com

About the Author

An Oxford modern languages graduate and prize-winning former journalist, Sarah was shortlisted in the Templar Poetry Pamphlet and Collection Competition 2009. *Into the Yell* is Sarah's first full-length collection but her work has been widely published in anthologies and literary journals, as well as online. Her individual poems and short stories have achieved success in numerous competitions and she has experience as a poetry competition adjudicator herself.

The 35 year old was poet in residence at Worcester's Oxfam Bookshop for National Poetry Day 2009 and is the Poetry Society's Worcester and Droitwich Stanza representative. She also runs writing workshops.

She currently lives in Worcestershire with her husband, two children, a battered laptop and hundreds of books.

www.sarah-james.co.uk

Into the Yell
Reviewers' Comments

Sarah James' poems are full of colour, a life-affirming response   to both the domestic and the fantastic. Nevertheless, they   are aware of darker shades, the grimmer side of life, relationships and the imagination. This is a varied, thought-provoking and enjoyable first collection.

Jacqui Rowe –
    Poetry Society Trustee and co-director of Flarestack Poets

Sarah James's poems are earthy, sensuous, often sexy, peopled by resonant characters, such as Shakespeare's Juliet and a stiletto-heel-wearing Inuit. Always clear-eyed and compassionate, she explores the visceral realities of the female body; the pain of infertility and post-natal depression with language that pins down her subject with surgical precision.

Catherine Smith –
>   award-winning poet and Poetry Book Society/Guardian
>   'next generation poet'.

Sarah James deciphers the world with a wise young eye; attentive to complexity, she makes her own sense of things - and expresses it in language that is often dramatic, and always engaging.

Meredith Andrea –
>   co-director of Flarestack Poets

Sarah James's first collection shows an imagination that can surprise and delight, as well as skill and confidence in her craft. I am already looking forward to seeing what she does next.

Angela France –
>   poet and features editor of *Iota*

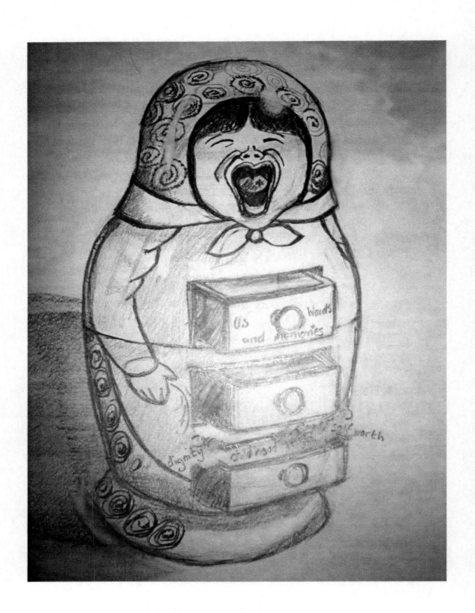

Editor's Introduction

I first came across Sarah James' work in the Earlyworks Press anthology, *Misfit Mirror*, which has two of her poems: 'Mandy Jones is Singing' and 'My Mother's Compact'. Both have become favourites of mine. So I was understandably pleased to be asked to help with editing Sarah's first collection of poetry. Although there was some initial nervousness on my part, never having done this kind of thing before, I did actually enjoy the months of pruning, shaping and ordering. And, despite a mutual tendency towards indecisiveness, I think we have put together a judiciously well-pruned, well-shaped, and well-ordered collection of poetry.

I began reading the bulky manuscript that eventually became *Into the Yell*, rather appropriately, at Dylan Thomas' boathouse in Laugharne over cups of tea and slices of bara brith, and was immediately impressed by the way that the poems, while exploring the serious afflictions of living, loving and dying, managed to include whiskered, wolfish grannies, a stiletto-wearing Inuit whose lover is a polar bear, and news that the Dalai Lama uses Twitter. Not only that, there was the reappearance of the incomparable Mandy Jones who, after much agonising, inspired the book's title.

At this stage it's hard to remember all those anxious, nail-biting, moments when we had to decide which poems should go and which should stay; how to start, and how to finish. *Into the Yell*, the end result of all those agonising decisions, now seems to have almost magically and painlessly emerged, its form somehow predetermined and absolutely right. I'm very proud to have had a role in the formation of such an amusing, intelligent and insightful collection of poetry.

Marilyn Francis January 2010

Dedication

For Justin, James and Daniel

Contents

Welcome to the Zoo

My name is Sarah and I am your guide
this morning, ladies and gentlemen, girls and boys.
Please keep all your belongings close
and please, please feed the animals.

I am the flea that drinks off skin and fur.
The fly on the wall is nothing to me.
I borrow other lives, try them for taste;
sip, suck, guzzle – then move on as I like.

Notice the peahen on your left, pruning her mate's colours:
helping him paint the air while she waits, watches,
follows him, dressed in the sweep
of his shadow; pecks dust.

I am the zebra with striking black bands
of text. My letters shine against white stripes.
Then I kick hooves; roll questions in the mud
until all of my writing is smeared and smudged.

Watch orangutan Mum cuddle her baby continuously
one whole year, slow-swing him through the trees,
nuzzle him to unbroken sleep in her nest
of playful, restless dreams.

I am the cochineal beetle who bleeds
ink willingly. I'd grind my own body
to find the answers; spell them out in red
while the cactus quill spears me as I write.

The reptile house is open today but
our lizards are cold-blooded, shy. With camouflage scales,
they'll hide behind stones, leaves, anything to avoid being seen.
They'll even shed their own tails to escape.

I am the snake; my coiled form an ear lobe.
My body bends sounds to words, words to sounds
in constant slither; still never, never
silent. Listen! Hear my heart's hissing tick.

The penguin's characteristic waddle may raise a laugh.
It walks nowhere fast but is a powerful
swimmer, reaching 9mph. Some say its wings
are a memory, or wish, of when it could fly.

I am the tiger. Stripes alight, my bright
eyes burn two holes in the night as I blaze
fearful forests with my gaze; search my self
for the slightest trace of symmetry.

Daffodil Trail

It starts on the grey, scuffed
pavement at the end of the drive:
a trail of squashed stars
pulled down to earth,
their long stems leaking green.

Better not to ask what happened.
There's a patch of rooty, bleeding
stubble left in the garden.
Someone has used a wax strip
to peel sun from the flowerbed.

Blue hyacinths froth,
red tulips stretch thin necks to the sky
and a leafy patchwork of primulas
cushions flat mud.
But someone has stolen the daffodils;

lifted them as lightly
as soiled hands plucked
childhood from the boys
who picked them, their fingers
stained with pollen.

My Sweet

Get off! she screams, dodging around trees.
A distant light gleams through wet leaves
but never seems nearer, only deeper out in the night.

Bramble fingers snatch fistfuls of hair, scratch
her clothes, pull at her mother's loose threads.
Her skin-thin coat bleeds scraps of red.

As her foot stubs a stone,
something hard hits her cheek. She falls,
feels purple-blue flowers creep up her legs.

Then they stop. She's silent, still, spilling with fear;
smells fox, damp, rotting wood, wants
to peel off the stench, wrench out thorns,

float into the sky hidden somewhere high
above shadows, beyond the hiss
of tall grass, the frog's croak, insect bites...

And now she's up, up, running again, heading
for the glow of her grandmother's house,
where *Help! Help!* awaits at last.

There, there, you'll be all right.
Let Nanna's love hug you close.
Don't stand on the doorstep, come on in!

Then her grandmother's grin gleams
all teeth, whispers,
Look, my sweet, a special treat!

The Un-Niceness of Nice

Caved four weeks into the hills with her,
her son, his woman, beans barely boiled,
steak sizzled, skins singed;
juiced red like the sun.

I scooped dust from melons, swept
flesh from floors, rectangled beds,
while the sun shook off the sweet
shade of trees; rained insects and figs.

One day free a week, I was dropped in the city:
Don't be swept off your feet, she hissed.
No men, miss! I remember her English
though I forget the son's French.

So I made like a lizard:
slipped into heat's skin, flicked out
my tongue, dribbled the red of his steak –
spit on my lips.

Second Year Notes on Molière

It's not man flu, you're not Argan,
you tell me when you call,
snuffling through holes in your breath.
I cycle over, find you
tucked up in bed, pale and creased.
Bleary-eyed, you growl
that you're only watching TV
cos you can't read a book,
can barely eat, let alone
make it to lectures.
You don't want to cause a fuss
but you could need a sick bowl
and of course I'll take notes for you.
But before I go...
You do look ill, I agree, fluffing the duvet,
bolstering your pillow round ruffled hair.
So I nip to the shop for bread and milk,
pick up tissues, a pack of your favourite throat sweets.
Back at your flat, I fetch the bits in,
wipe round your shared kitchen,
heat some tinned soup,
offer it on a clean tray.
You sip tentatively,
say you can't quite stomach the taste,
though you swallow the sweets,
ask me to rustle up buttered toast.
I bring jam too, an opened packet of plain digestives
(no doubt a housemate's)
and lean over to kiss you goodbye, already late.
You don't feel hot but it must
be the tablets kicking in,
you explain with a sniff.
My nose itches
at the whiff of dead lager.

Studying 'Villains'

The word always makes me think of France.
I've said it now but, racist
though it may appear at first,
I find the letters remind me of 'ville'
– and after all towns villain nature;
bleed out light with concrete leeches.
Then there's Villon and his medieval version of French,
which changes, as languages and villains do,
from century to century, context to con-text.
(NB Remember villains, like linguists,
aren't always as clever as they think!)
But what I learnt most as a student
living in the echo of Rouen's l'hôtel de ville,
deciphering my parents' divorce
from a series of late-night phone calls
and schizophrenic hand-scrawled letters,
is the deception of words
and how quickly unmasked love
turns heroes to villains.

The Rain in Rouen

It's different on holiday: patchwork of quaint cobbles,
colours of Monet's Garden, framed by sun.
You don't notice grey flowers, slipping on wet stone.

Four years there; she swirls the city's vowels
round her mouth like vin rouge but can't roll them out right,
any more than she can roll a Rizla.

Instead, she puffs a thin Gitane, tries to look chic
as she sips café noir on the brasserie pavement splashed
by a culture she can only borrow.

No Au Revoir

This time will be the last
ferrying from one familiar to another.

All she can see now are shades
of water. And movement.

Nothing is still. It's hard to focus half-way
between two countries; moving horizons

of sea and sky. But she can still hear
her apartment sigh, friends laugh, heels tap

half-moons into laminate. She feels
her bare feet on metal steps spiralling

into the sky above Place de la Rougemare
and tries to loose goodbyes from the roof like doves.

But the words tie themselves up in French knots
tingling the tip of her tongue.

I don't believe in feng shui but...

I chose those curtains for the colour:
blood orange, the hot embers of a fire,
red wine, the inside curve of your mouth,
that silk lining of closed eyelids
satiated with love. Or so I hoped.
The black script pattern was purely practical:
its matching linen wouldn't show marks.
Manufacturers called the coordinated set
'Feng Shui in Red', though the only thoughts
I'd given to space and lay-out
were how to fit in a single bed,
silk sheets (clichéd but oh, so sensual),
a thick rug to velvet bare feet
and enough cushions and pillows
to stop us bumping heads
on the bedstead mid-way
through the passion I imagined.
It was only the morning after that I wondered
whether it was such a good idea,
considered the curtains
and what those bedspread symbols meant.
Ancient proverbs about wise men's need for sleep,
an oriental love story,
Chinese 'Jabberwocky' or
(some bored designer having a laugh)
the sinographic script for "fuck" ?

Cold Fingers

When your necklace broke, spilling
its heart, I bought you a new one in gold.

You chucked the old chain into a drawer
scented with the lavender of unwanted gifts.

Now, sorting through bits you left behind, I find it dangling
from a CD case: Enya's *Paint the Sky with Stars*.

I feel your hair plaited into metal links, try not
to think of cold fingers

on your neck; unfastening.

Chemistry Finals

An atheist, Tom still grew faith in his beard,
like Samson. He convinced himself
wisdom, or his revision at least,
was linked to his lengthening stubble.
Cu, Ag, Mg, Fe – elements bristled his chin,
each strand strengthened with learning,
exploded in a fuzz of equations:
his knowledge – and salvation maybe –
coiled in the cocoon of a
dandelion clock.

The Harry Lime Society

In my dreams, I still paint sheep pink,
then string them from our neighbour's trees
like knobbly, fluffy, kicking fruit.

Then next-door's students shear the ewes, rip
up the turf from our much prized lawn,
replace it with strips of lime-dyed wool.

Shorn sheep amble from our grounds to theirs
and back again, pooing and chewing,
chewing and pooing the long grass of college rivalry.

The Inuit Who Couldn't Give Up Heels

At breakfast her stilettos stabbed
dented moons in the morning snow.

She hated disco but pole danced
every night in the igloo she shared with a bear;

her cigarette smouldering star holes in the roof,
bare legs fishnetted with snowflakes.

This was not for show, though everyone looked,
but to blend her skin to the landscape; freeze

clumsy telltale motion. While she waited,
she pinned her mouth closed with icicles.

Her mate, the bear, kept watch for give-away
signs while she waited,

               hushed. Every month her hopes bled
white with the unlush silence of snowfall.

While she waited – pale flamingo, mid-
pirouette – for a flash of life under the ice,

the red of her heels speared more fish
than two of them could eat.

The Inuit Who Wouldn't Wear Her Slippers

They fitted. But she feared the glass might shatter.
Besides, where would she wear them?
Fishing, the gas station, to tea with the penguins?

And balls were what sea lions balanced
for princely tourists in far away zoos.
Instead, she placed the slippers

on her bedside cabinet;
kept them clean, polished
with a soft cloth so she could see

her dreams reflect unsmeared
first thing in the morning
and last thing at night as she fell asleep:

bare legs, bare arms, bare breasts
but feet completely covered;
their soles heeled with ice.

Unsubmerged

In Dominica, an earthquake cracked
Roger's home like a walnut.
His wife's omelette pan skipped off the stove,
their bed hopped the floor, chairs
pirouetted into shaking walls.
But cotted snug in a box for their breakfast –
half a dozen eggs, unbroken.

Visiting his mother in Grenada,
a hurricane peeled her house like an orange.
Winds stacked roofs, turned
tamarind trees into mops, uprooted
nutmeg plantations but left the glass
of his daughter's portrait a smooth,
unrippled ocean.

Half-submerged in New Orleans, Roger's shoes
walked in pairs on water. Tables arked,
chairs waded out the doors
and dead rats trailed the apartment stairs,
while his daughter's dress
hung freshly pressed on her bedroom door:
dry and pink with flowers.

Juliet's Last Letter

Dear Son, There are some things you should
know about me and your father, Romeo.
Ours was not a fling, no
flash in the pan —
whatever others may come to say.
He was my man: the consonants
that framed my name,
the vowels of music in between.
But the sins of fathers tighten round hearts.
How I love my family, yet
their name scalds my tongue,
clenches my throat,
would try to cleave the sun in two.
Paris is a good man also but not
my man. He would marry me for others' sakes,
proudly raise you as his son,
make you his heir.
But the softness of your cuckooed nest
would be lined with nettles and dandelion clocks.
Oh my unnamed child with bones bent
from wishes and a heartbeat of sighs!
Even when I dream, my lips on your forehead
offer a poisoned kiss.
Oil separates from water
in the apothecary's magic potions
and knowledge has its own motion: a clot
circling your borrowed father's spleen,
the bee-sting that would tingle my skin and swell
with the irritation of learned love's rouge.
Better, I fear, to wrap you now in a blanket
of herbs and bindweed
than watch you live to grow
into the lie no one forgives...

Barren

Tuna mayonnaise does it for Claire, or vinaigrette;
bubbles of oil suspended miraculously
in the mix. Like fertilised eggs pipetted into a petri dish
those days when she'd have thanked any man
who could grant her wish for children:
make emptiness not her fault; shoulder the blame.

Worlds away, a suncaked woman balances water,
shoulders hollowed-out cravings

Want triumphant now, Claire craves sugar
and salt, yearns for scones with jam,
freshly churned cream, the smell of warm bread.
Hunched head over hard belly, she sniffs
clenched fists crammed with dough,
face glowing fertility.

Hunger crouches in vinegar mud as stick lips pray
for a baby daughter bartered for food

Claire is all stocked up; prepared beyond reason.
Minimalist kitchen shelves burst
with boxes, cartons, packets, tins...
Next to milk and nappies, untouched
onions soak up acid in a pickling jar, expand
like her waist; swell with excess.

Haemogoblin

Doctors sum up her loss in a plummeting
language of numbers.
They can't figure out how
she's strong enough to stand:
her haemoglobin's all wrong.
And her haemo-goblin?
That premature pixie thing in its trolley box?
But she must concentrate.
Her heart rate is fast, reactions slow.
Tablets won't help iron it out –
she needs a transfusion.
Red plastic is pumped into her arm
through a kite string too slack to fly,
while the grounded blanket wails
and rings still won't fit her stubby fingers;
fat cigars smoked
not to the baby's arrival
or the replacement of her lost life blood.
No, hot embers scar her arm
with the pain of something she's missing.

Bitter Pill

This is the pill that helps me love my baby.
Even before his birth, the bad fairy cast her spell.
Nothing can break it. Not willpower, not wishing.

Nine long months I carefully spun the yarn
of his life before the needle pricked me,
bled me of the love of motherhood.

But one day, someone, something must
hack through the numbness
of this thorny curse, cleave

my need to swallow this bitter pill
and wake me from such deep, uneasy sleep
before my prince has grown too tall.

Instrumental

He is almost an orchestra –
air flute, trombone, guitar. His fat
fingers pluck the beat from thin air.

A one-boy band of *Bohemian Rhapsody*,
Flash Gordon, Ziggy Stardust and the Spiders from Mars.
Words slither over him unabsorbed. But

music surges through his cells
in a flow of electrical charge:
strum bass, air organ, drum roll

cartwheeling him rock style onto his back
with a wild fandango of limbs
that twangs the strings of my heart.

Ungrounded

I choose a big blue four, sure he'll be pleased.
He bobs the balloon proudly,
then hugs the gas cushion to his chest and
pulls its string loose.
We watch it drift tailless out of sight.
He smiles.
                    Ribbon trails
from the loop around his wrist.
He tugs and stretches its knot free, passes
the slip-stream to me.
Thank you, I say; hear
even my words float away from him
as I wind his birthday ribbon so tight
that untied blue bruises my hand.

Pink

They're gathered at the school gate:
six haloed flamingos,
long-legged and elegant,
all feathers and flounce.

They eye up the other mothers
from the loop-necked height
of their immaculate grooming,
comparing manicured beaks.

I penguin-flap past their chopstick legs,
pinch a single pink feather, unnoticed,
as they're stood wings outstretched,
preening their perfection.

In the Garden

Snow on twigs reminds her of Nanna's knitted shawl;
the whiskers on her grandmother's chin bristling through wool,
false teeth glinting moonlight.
                                         But it was daytime:

mocking birds singing, singing birds mocking
the naïve skip of her heart and feet
weaving the trees.

Shift angle with the sunlight
and her red cape's abandoned
like a pool of blood
                            slicking the grass.

Nanna's house is empty,
weeps fur from its door;
a silver blade is sunk in mud. No

hint then of the constant noise:
the aching chop, chop of the woodcutter's axe
which now hacks through her head.

She prefers the garden at night,
densely dark like the forest, almost quiet
but for the wolf that howls her dreams.

nightmare rising

a new calf on stilts, i
wade through the shock of
night-rising, stumble-

pad downstairs as shadow rocks
leach from the lamp
left on like a lighthouse

to warn of nightmares,
whose patterns now melt
into wallpaper flowers, seep

away through carpet
as the chill of kitchen tiles
fishnets my legs

i feel cold
skin exposed;
dark watching

Awaking to the weight
of daytime expectations, I
curtain bare moon windows.

Double Bluff

Clubs, diamonds, hearts, spades.
When they met, he was chasing the ace
to amuse her best friend's children.
His preferred game is Texas hold'em,
though his natural luck stops short,
runs only to jack high.
But he's good at bluffing;
reducing speech to a flatline,
turning rooms into a vacuum,
sucking up everyone's breath.
Even now, after ten years, she can't tell.
When he phones to say he's working late,
she's never sure which way to bet
though she looks for tell-tale signs:
sidling eyes, shadowed smile,
perfume of booze, scent, lipstick.
All she can smell is aftershave,
and the hint of something else, undefinable.
He promised once he would stop.
But you can't change the marks on the cards.
A seven's always a seven, a heart's a heart.
If she'd been dealer, she'd have shuffled better.
At worst, she'd have more odds on her side:
a stronger position to decide whether
to fold or raise.

Daisy Chain

You made me a daisy chain
of promises: *love, trust, fidelity...*
each threaded with a long-stemmed kiss.

I hung it round my neck,
touched it every day, afraid
its fragile links might break

or the flowers – deprived
of roots, soil, water –
curl and close their sunshine eyes.

As I leave,
the split stalks drip
petal tears.

The Silence of Painting

Her single brush stroke flickers
like a candle flame; expands sometimes
so she fills the whole canvas:
subject, foreground, background, frame...
Then it shrinks back
into a solitary dot.

Oil textures expressively; but its shine is heavy,
movement thick and sticky.
She should have chosen aquarelle
perhaps; water has little colour
except the tones it reflects.
Sea mimics sky.

But it isn't the colour or lack of colours
which appeals to her:
it is the painting's silence.

Friends joke that her self-portrait is lean,
call it 'minimalist'.
The therapist suggests she add a stroke a day.

She doesn't tell him that she tries
but every night someone washes it clean.

Expectation

Poetry patterns magnolia walls;
voices lilting in and out
between silences, clapping,
the murmur of bridge next door.

Later, we leave drunk
on rhythms and images,
stumbling through the lounge that
reminds us of an old people's home
– furnished with faded floral chairs,
sticks and clock hands fumbling.

We trail dalmation spots
down partly redecorated stairs, throw
ourselves out into the dusk.

Driving home, alloy eyes vibrate towards us
from herringboned skies.
We pass power station geysers,
decide to return via the visiting fair.

Sliding from trousers to jeans
in the dark of a car park, I gasp
at my middle-aged daring, expect
streets spilling with music,
lights spinning excitement.

But when we get there, the fair
is smaller than my imagination.
Streets spin with cacophony,
lights spill youth's disappointment;
yearn for the shape of magnolia walls.

Your Suicide Note

It's time for my retinopathy 'scan'.
The man ticks off questions, tells me tip
my head back, look at the ceiling.
I search the white
as later he will search my retinas.
But before I find any answers,
he drips a drop in my left eye, then my right.
I weep, hope he will see nothing there;
wonder if that's what you saw.
Returning to the waiting room,
I continue to search my memory
for signs: intonations
tangled between the lines,
double meanings I sliced too thinly.
My vision mists; a clingfilm smudge.
Poster warnings blur to unshaped colour,
buzz with the broken-up words
of your brief final note.
I imagine your breath on the bathroom mirror,
then its sudden clearing.
Winter sunlight submerges the room.
I hope the man calls my name soon,
before your answer blinds me.

No Referral

My ophthalmology results arrive by post nine days later:
the photograph shows only minor eye changes
(some background retinopathy is expected).

The screening manager adds a few advisory notes
but there's no referral, just an invitation
to return routinely in one year's time.

I wedge the letter in peripheral vision,
next to a friend's psychologist card
and a pile of your unforwarded bills.

French Manicure

Tidy up your nail extensions, yes?

The Parisian beautician flits her emery board
like a violin bow across my fingers.

The big do tonight? You have a pretty dress?

She pushes back cuticles, snips dry skin, flicks
her file along each side, rounds corners.

Lengthen the hand, see. You be the belle of ball.

I imagine myself shimmying the room without you;
belly sucked in, blisters puffing the ball of my foot.

Maybe you meet one new man...That's okay?

The girl shapes, buffs, files, infills,
infills, buffs; polishes false nails to perfection.

You have the good time, yes.

I pay; shaping real conversations with you in my head
while I buff my smile like acrylic.

The Tree Surgeon Warned

It was a season of growth:
the business boasted record profits
and we sipped champagne on the patio,
toasting our first grandchild.

Spring bulbs burst garden borders,
daisies leaked across the lawn.
Our almond tree blossomed into a giant bridal bouquet,
later clogging drains with confetti.

My favourite tree, Dad once told me it grew memories
and its branches held up the sky.
I laughed, burrowing its bark into my back
as sun tanned my skin mahogany.

But that was childhood: the tree younger, sun softer.
Forty years later, rubbing almond oil
into forget-me-knots climbing my legs,
I found a mole on my thigh had flowered.

Shades of black had opened out petal edges,
spreading pollen growth across my body.
The almond shed its white blossom:
flakes of dead skin on the grass.

That week a tree surgeon warned
the roots threatened our foundations;
it needed felling immediately.
My sky was about to fall.

Human Tumours

They're all sitting patiently,
or not. Some have been here longer than others.
She tries to read the signs.
On - call - oh - gee!
It's infectious – this sick humour
that limps round the waiting room.

She watches, guesses who's here for what.
Relative, friend or patient?
Some are easy to diagnose:
bandanas and caps a dead give-away.

Her morbid fascination
distracts better than flicking
through the gloss of celebrity pictures.

She creates whole lives,
invents families, hospital records;
decides their fate for no reason except to pass time,
kill thinking and,
if she's lucky,
slip into someone else's successful recovery.

Soundscape

Waking to the smell of salt, taste of sand,
she hears rustle of sea and leaves,
muffled thuds of distant movement
and staccato tapping of water in pipes.

Hugging the warmth of her cardigan,
she feels strong for once and stands up,
looking away from faded B & B cleanliness
to sip, sip a whisper of stillness from the beach.

Inhaled colours: pink, orange, yellow
hint at island heather, gorse, cloudy shrubs...
This shimmering lullaby of sky and sea
soothes with the *sh, sh* of a mother's presence.

Maybe this time she is better.
She tries to photograph the semblance of tranquillity
but a figure cycles past on the coastal road:
noisy black shape etched forever on her Turner landscape.

The echo of its metallic clink-clank stains
the untouched softness, scratches:
sand on skin or rope around her neck.
The sea's childhood lisp hisses now: *This is it!*

So she waits; stretching across silence to listen
for the tide's triumphant crescendo —
or the hush of shallow sea breath
curled into a shell.

Slivers

For their anniversary, he brings roses she can't see,
dribbling scent she can't share.

A nurse slips the thin stalks into water
while he daubs his wife's seamed lips
with Vaseline, uses a borrowed
baby brush to unbramble her hair.
Then, sitting beside her, stifled
more by the artificial light
than the summer sun behind the blinds,
he sips plastic tea, nibbles a wafer.

He wishes he could bring her tastes,
share the crunch of his biscuit...

Slivers of time melt on his tongue,
taste buds unearth memories
buried like fossils between thin strata.
He smells grass on her fingers, remembers
rolling down a hill, her voice tickling,
feather-soft hair on his face,
strawberries oozing juice, her mouth unpicked and
sweet as chocolate.

6am at the Pool

He swims upright, like a sea-horse
curved rigid at the neck
always looking down to the depths

water corals him: he
refuses the still specimen jar
solidified frigid

his vertical paddle is a real crawl
but movement is movement
even if slight; clawing

The Last Thing To Do Before You Die: Ten Options

Flash across a football pitch
being filmed for national telly.
Have sex on the beach with a stranger.
Paint your fingernails orange,
plait tinsel into your hair, tattoo
a Christmas tree on your bum.
Create a giant statue
of two glass fingers stuck in the air.
Borrow your ex's Ferrari,
hit 160 down the M1.
Take tea with the clouds on Everest.
Break your own best 4-minute mile.
Kiss your kids goodbye.
Try to forget you'll never remember it.
Smile!

My Mother's Compact

It was a present for her twenty-first:
metal sheen still untarnished
when she gave it to me.
The lid's golden petals looked expensive.

I carried it but didn't use it.
The mirror's smallness cut my face
into pieces: nose, eye, mouth, eye.
My breath evaporated them all.

One night at a party, I watched some girl sniff
at her reflection in a plain mirror
laid flat enough to skate on,
scuffed ice on its surface.

When I got home, my compact was gone.
I imagined it drowning in melted snow
or in some pawn shop abandoned open-mouthed:
an oyster mourning its pearl.

Through the Kitchen Window

March sunshine catches my eye.
A black smear marks her kitchen window but
normally I wouldn't notice.
Today, I'm forced to see things
Mother's way.
Outside, flowers dance
brightly but I can't shrug off my winter greyness.
The furnished rooms echo
a familiar emptiness.
I remember it starting every year:
her own obsessive behaviour.
She'd iron curtains, spring-clean
the corner of the corner of cupboards.
I look at the kitchen window,
for signs of her presence.
My heart searches
for her handprint on the glass.
I reach out and feel
March sunshine warming my fingers,
I see a sand martin sing daffodil yellow.

I see a sand martin sing daffodil yellow.
March sunshine warming my fingers,
I reach out and feel
for her handprint on the glass.
My heart searches
for signs of her presence.
I look at the kitchen window,
the corner of the corner of cupboards.
She'd iron curtains, spring-clean
her own obsessive behaviour.
I remember it starting every year:
a familiar emptiness.
The furnished rooms echo
brightly but I can't shrug off my winter greyness.

Outside, flowers dance
Mother's way.
Today, I'm forced to see things
normally I wouldn't notice.
A black mark smears her kitchen window but
March sunshine catches my eye.

Remembrance

It's eleven o'clock in the pool:
even the red of floats and beaded ropes
won't stretch to the metaphor
of poppy fields; or rivers of blood.

In a locker, my paper poppy's pinned down
like a butterfly wing to folded clothes:
out of sight, away from light.
It cannot grow; or die.

I gash the water with my body, splash
the silence, break through thin bars
of sunlight from the blinds.
In my imagination, the space fills with gas

not water: frantic children thrashing
front crawl through poisonous air;
their parents watching, choking on love
before fumes choke them.

And still my poppy can neither grow nor die
but lies in the locker with a pin
that stings my finger but pricks
only a hint of blood.

Chlorine nettles my eyes;
in my ears, the muffled buzz of doodlebugs,
echo of marching, screams, squealing bombs.
I dive through waves of crumpled bodies.

In the locker now, my paper poppy's dissolving,
clothes unfolding, grasping for air.
Their anguished sobs rattle the sides;
shake our silence.

'Spa Man'

Daytime he's just a statue poised mid-
dive. But at night tensed wooden muscles
spear down, crack open the earth.
Spartan, naked in his autumn leaf tan,
he plunges through mud to drill for brine;
unlayers time to look for his lady —
the spa nymph whose saline tongue
still stings his dreams.
Only owls listen now
as he howls out her name; longs
to kiss life into brineless lips.
But his mouth chokes on dry dirt, swallows history.
Grainy tears seep flowers and soil with salt.

Cumulus

Even before they met, Thomas collected clouds;
he could taste rain on his tongue
simply by looking at the right sky.

He'd greet each formation like his sheep,
whistling as he recognised its unique shape and mix
of white, grey, black; individual as every new lamb.

Cirrus, altocumulus, cumulonimbus...Betsy, Pippa, Lou...
He'd recite names, munching syllables like marshmallows,
while his sheep munched methodically

through mud-stained grass, only stopping
to collect under trees by the gate
when a nimbostratus threatened rain.

They'd huddle there as if hoping,
like her, for a cumulus
big enough to carry them far away.

Instead, spring lambs gave birth to winter ewes
and the weather brought more woolly skies.
Rain collected regularly in buckets, overflowing

across the farm's loose-tiled kitchen,
where the air tasted of mildew
and she grew tired of waiting.

Naked

He loves
her from his bench:
open lips, black hole eyes,
spider leg lashes, firm arse, long
curled snake.

Curled snake
lunges from grass.
Tattooed tongue flicks coils, forked
lick: kiss for her, for him a hiss.
He tastes.

He tastes
apple and peach
in her hair, hint of ink
charming the beast from her hips to
his mouth.

His mouth
slips into hers.
She leaves. He doesn't grieve
but can't peel the feel of her from
his life.

His life
starts and ends there:
one night at the pub, glass
of snakebite, pint of bitter, then
naked.

Naked
is not his thing.
No sin — but he can't shed
the reptile scales from his skin when
he loves.

Tapestry

Grandmother's cottage could be fairytale –
thatched with satin dreams, French knotted
with flowers and the red of your coat. But

you'd still hanker after cross-stitch,
leave working the snow till last –
scared the wool, rougher than fur or flakes,

might blizzard out your wolf or
the skeins stain with sweat,
reveal reality's touched whiteness.

For Sale

The nuns left today.
It's taken a fortnight to move
all their earthly belongings;
pack the last 170 years into a van.
Mother Abbess says they'll need days
to unstack the boxes at Wass,
North Yorkshire, 200 miles away.
But that it seems is God's plan.
Behind them, leaf shadows swarm
the chapel like flies, flutter
light at the gardener's feet.
His boots clatter the cobbles
while the caretaker prays
to a sale sign, worships dust.
It could take years to
unclutter this emptiness.

Poole's Cavern, Buxton: An Unofficial Tour

It's dark inside the dinosaur's head
though its skull gleams white in the guide's torchlight
swallowed thousands of years deep within the earth.

We enter in reverse – through the intestines first;
voices stoop, echo the empty shell
of this rocky skeleton.

The taste of excitement draws us closer into the bare
hole of its belly where melted bones
drip from the roof in spikes.

This is not Jonah's whale though perhaps
they are not dissimilar. There's no fishy odour
but we can feel damp scales.

Cold carves crosses into our backs
and we shiver with reverence,
sense the secret of the Earth's beginning...

Here, beauty meets bile in repulsive shudder:
blue-grey fungi climb monster ribs,
inverted nipples, black-headed warts, orange mould.

Among white-tinged villi, remnants of the monster's dinner
lie caked in limestone and calcite:
a dragon's head, elephant's trunk, crouching cat.

We continue onwards through the beast's inner organs,
past where Mary Queen of Scots once stood
and beyond the bats, eight steps down to the cavern behind its eyes.

A decaying cauliflower sits solidified on its tongue poised
mid-taste; still feasting, like us,
on the miracle of time's mineral mysteries.

The Coldest Winter for More than a Decade

They're not flakes but flowers:
a flurry of winter blossom
from stratocumulus bushes.

The sun is the sky's
single squashed fruit –
warm heart of the snow's sloppy kiss.

Discussing the weather then Darwin,
my husband says
humans used to hibernate.

Otherwise they'd have frozen in awe.

Deluge

Flowers tip tap glockenspiel petals on my windows:
a soft yet insistent plea to come in.

Soon they start creeping under doors: carpet
of tulips, daffs and primulas.

Outside, birds sip from giant mud bowls,
watch as my garden migrates to the warmth inside.

Wallpaper swirls with leaves and broken stems:
this living room no longer mine but nature's —

with armchair flowerbeds, plant pot cushions
and a sofa paisleyed in cabbage and peas.

The Mariner's Mistake

It had been a long voyage for the crew
through shuddering horizons, salty sleep,
stormy dreams and hungry squalls.

For weeks, winds had lashed their backs,
slapped cheeks swollen like sails,
while rotten food fermented mutinous fumes.

Then, at last, land: grass, the flatness of home...
Tiles replaced sky, sunsets were not dying light
but the colour of flowers scenting wives' hair.

Alas, the captain had barely heard of the Semper Augustus,
never dreamed Dutch merchants would pay a king's ransom
for something that looked like a vegetable.

His error was costly,
lost him his ship laden with goods
when he undervalued his cargo; mistook

his tulip bulb for an onion,
made it his celebratory landing supper,
surprising his palate

– unforewarned by tearless peeling –
with the taste of spring, bees, honey...
a faint metallic taint of money.

Laser Bullets

It's on TV again: half-nanny state warning,
half-Nostradamus prediction.

I think of black oceans, tsunami waves
and desert islands prone to storms
when it snows scorched earth.
We will live off landfill, concreted
underground in carrier bag tents.
Even the fake trees will lose
their plastic leaves.

My six year old asks what's for tea
and *Mum, when will Earth explode?*

I think he imagines a ringside seat,
complete with pop, hotdog and chips.
There's a fanfare or gunshot sparking
the biggest fireworks he's ever seen.
Then it's colours whizzing and fizzing,
stars charring bright holes in the sky
or a comet tail blazing laser bullets

which shoot down the world bang-hiss while
pixels of ash burst from our screen.

The Last Courtyard

The worms went quickly,
then the birds turned.
They pecked crumbs of mortar,
toothpicked brickwork until
the courtyard of song and scent was lichen-bare.
Sown seeds ungrown, bread dead,
hunger dug in. Eyes gleamed
like berries to be beaked.
Wounded, chicks and hens were first:
flesh sucked through hollow claws.
Those left used the legs as sticks.
They gulped brushed lavender
from dry stone fountains,
then turned like worms upon themselves,
choked sound with plucked-out feathers
and buried their own bones
in this scentless courtyard of echoes.

Jack of All Trades

It takes ten thousand hours
to reach 'expert' status –
or so my friend's husband told her
someone figured on some
documentary he'd watched.
Apparently, it applies to anything.
So ten years' writing...my poetic hope
does the maths and sighs.
Some apprenticeship
when careers change faster than seasons!
In any case, what counts?
Where do reading, researching, editing fit
in this complex equation?
Sounds more like algebra
than writing, I say.
More formulaic than creative,
my friend agrees. She grins.
Cos if 10 (x + y) = 10,000 /w,
where does that leave u?

My Perfect Lover

His voice will leave millipede tracks
up my spine, curl round my breasts,
hang in a necklace of long vowels.

I will bite off final consonants,
nibble his syllables from both ends
until sound explodes on my tongue.

And when he leaves, as lovers do,
his words will linger inside,
echoing the beat of my heart.

Sex at the 'Randolph'

They're four floors up, glass case open
to cranes and Ashmolean shadows.

His archaeologist fingers delve bed sheets;
unearth artefacts and exhibits.

Her breasts dangle like dry leather purses
aged by sun and soil acidity.

Does he imagine them catalogued, labelled;
poor examples from some Anglo-Saxon dig?

*Mammae dated circa 2008: note
the worn herringbone stitch across their surface.*

And when they're done will he turn back to facts,
sifting soil, the chemistry of carbon dating?

Perhaps he will jot her down in his log –
a few observations summing them up forever.

The professor's body shifts; flesh calcifies,
muscles mould into old stone building.

Debugging

Please step in front of the screen
and plug yourself in
so we can start deep cleaning.
It will be done in a flash.
One, two...searching
love drive for viruses.
Three, four...deleting dead emotions,
reprogramming memory.
Five, six...latex skin renewed,
LCD bruises erased.
Seven, eight...quick system check.
Nine, ten...reboot completed:
every circuit re-pulsed
in your electronic heart.

Missing Mantra

The Dalai Lama is following my husband.
We know it's true because Twitter told him so.
It's not often one gets an email like that.
Take note. We've made the new message
sound our mantra,
listen to it tick-tock time in the office,
chant lullabies into my sleep,
while my husband sits up in the dark
polishing his grit of wisdom
in the hope he'll create a pearl.

Escape

Inspired by a newspaper print of Dorothea
Tanning's 'Eine Kleine Nachtmusik' 1943.

i)

The sunflower is grounded:
a squashed star tugged
down to earth by the tangle
of seaweed girls coiled in its roots,
drugged, tantrum-tired. Weighted.

Green walls close dark doors
as she slips, sleep-like, out
through the one lit crack,
leaves her skin trailing the stairs
like a discarded stocking.

ii)

she exits the picture backwards, climbs
naked down the next page's text,
where she squeezes, emaciated,
between constricting letters –
black bruise
of conformity –
until she is out of print,
no smudge trace of
bare feet on the jaundiced paper
now she can sprint

Fault Lines

Her fingers itch. Vein ridges crack
in earthquake rifts, dead
lizard scales flake white debris.

She's never suffered this before.
Her mood swings seismograph style,
hand shakes as she rings her twin in San Francisco.

They haven't spoken for years
but used to connect without words –
and something must be causing her broken skin.

She imagines the earth's crust splitting
into a scar the length of the San Andreas Fault
– A dangerous place to live, she warned her sister.

She's missed her, of course she's missed her,
can't now remember the row
that crescendoed into silence.

Only that they couldn't agree
who was to blame about this or that;
wouldn't cede fault.

No answer. She puts down the phone,
turns on the television, where nothing is new:
the world still round, faults buried and unbroken.

But her breath tremors faster, fingers peel...
She goes to the doctor,
doesn't mention her twin

as he examines skin and breathing, prescribes
some cream and protective gloves.
Don't worry now, he says. *It's just eczema and*

mild panic attacks maybe.
Nothing broken. Then he frowns
as her heartbeat quakes the room.

Infectious

It got them in the GP's waiting room.
All they were doing was sitting there patiently.
He had an appointment to see the nurse
for his Moroccan holiday jabs.
She had called to collect her repeat prescription
but the doctor requested a quick chat first
to tick his routine boxes.

There wasn't much to do while waiting:
the usual 'nanny' notices,
a peacock's tail of creased gossip mags.
They both remembered to use
the touch-screen hand wash booking in
but she forgot healthy caution
reading the warning:
"Do not turn off. Plug to the fish tank."
Her fingers lingered in his glass handprint.

The reaction was immediate:
raised temperature, dry mouth,
heartbeat skiing the Alps.

It was an unconventional start;
this heady mix of love and germs.
When the doctors heard,
they washed their hands of the affair,
declared the surgery was not a meeting place,
dismissed rumours it might be catching.

But she still tore up her prescription,
ditched the fluoxetine pills
for a double dose of TLC.

Blinded

The woman who made snow globes
was blind. She stole lives and rolled
them up in glass balls.

There's an art to seeing small.
Her fingers pinpointed tiny details in wire,
built teeth monoliths, made paperclip trees.

She nipped flies' wings, dyed them leaf-green,
bent blunted needles into swings,
curved earrings for flowers.

Her people were fleshed from sewing pins.
She gave them no eyes, no faces
but plaited miniature skirts

from auburn strands of her neighbour's hair,
carefully collected by wetting her thumb with spit
and brushing it across the dancer's

pink sweater. A damp, unnoticed
cashmere kiss to which soft fibres
and glossy curls would stick.

Every night she would shake each globe,
water the scenes in coal-ash snow,
then warm up the glass with her hands.

The Bridesmaids of Port-au-Prince

*"...the people live side by side with livestock but take great
pride in keeping themselves clean." (From a report
by Alex von Tunzelmann, The Sunday Times, 17 May 2009.)*

Teenage girls in heels stilt Haiti's streets,
follow muddy slum sows,
scavenge scraps of urban love.

Their younger sisters wade human waste,
trade decomposing rubbish;
refuse to wallow in origami shacks.

Every night they return to the rust
of corrugated debts, clean
each other up with broken flowers –

lay out tomorrow's communion dress.

Dear Ellie,

i I can still write, see

Though the pen's borrowed and my sentences
sometimes slur, break off mid...
It's been a while but I know it's your birthday.
If I were rich, I would buy you jewels.
Instead I fashion words into gold charms,
wish you a life different from mine.

ii The Northern Line

A couple stomp on, mid-argument, at Camden Town.
Don't make a scene! she hisses loudly at his rigid back.
We all look away, pretend not to see.

At Euston, a mother drags on suitcase and screaming toddler.
Stop it! she shrieks. *Everyone's staring!*
We all look away, pretend not to hear.

Near Leicester Square, I stagger to my feet;
pretend not to mind the silence as I mutter,
Spare any change?

They all look away, pretend not to notice.

70

iii Poet on the Underground

I see him looking: a sneaky peek
at me, then back to his book –
Blake's *Songs of Innocence and Experience*,
his jottings in the margin.

Eyes flit up to a poster poem, glance
at my carrier of clinking bottles,
skim the grubby stub of my fingers, presume...
His hand moves down to note again.

Then those poetic eyes return to the verse.
He smiles. Is it
enjoyment, inspiration or pride?
Maybe his writing is on the wall.

All I know is I once knew things too.
Now my shoes drag unstitched tongues
along dusty pavements, dribble
my words into the cold night air.

iv P.S. I love you

I don't know how to sign this off,
can't tell when or where it ends.
But for now I leave you this letter
as my poem on the tube...

Letters

We break the word apart.
You easily picture each phoneme:
'h' is your grandad out of breath,
his hand raised to cough;
'e' is for eggs, broken in half;
then a vertical tongue flicks up to lick a lolly;
'p' is puffed cheeks
blowing out your seven birthday candles.

The-sounds-hop-scotch-to-the-end-of-your-tongue-then-stop,
fail to flow together.
We try again. I separate letters, pause,
urge you to have a go.
You-mi-mic-me-per-fect-ly-then-stop,
                                        stumbling on understanding
with the same staccato limp
that reminds me of my English professor
who had motor neurone disease;
his jerk-y movements
                    – clum-sy muscle spasms
jolt-ed my youthful impatience.

Your face pleads to me: open, hopeful...
I remember my own class at high school,
the girl from the farm.
"Thick as pig shit," we used to jeer in the playground.
She would milk cows, muck out horses,
pick strawberries all summer,
then sit up for hours with books
that must have read like 'Jabberwocky'.
Your face conflates with hers: open, hopeful...
                            My heart muscles spasm.

Mandy Jones is Singing

5am buzzes. Tired fingers fumble size sixteen jeans,
pull ivory across her eyes' blue hollows,
brush and fluff the fuzzy refrain of her hair.

It's shift time: grey light, grey metal, grey mops
– plastic and spongy, not the string-wigged
wooden mop of her childhood microphone.

She looks in the mirror, sees orange
street lamps blur the glass to a disco-light dazzle.
The young woman who stares back

has hair in long, silk crescendos
and a size ten figure in a pop star dress.
If only Mandy knew how to step through...

Into the Yell

Mandy's lover forces open her soprano mouth
with a dentist's grip
to search for sound.

Or not. Her closed throat
hides the secret of a voice whose shout
even is music pouring

                      out for others:
her soul, love, skies, birds,
the essence of human desires.

Perhaps he imagines extracting
that perfect vibration. A small slit
of a cut and he could

pull out her vocal cords for himself
like plucking strings.
Or gutting a rabbit.

Whatever he is looking for, it is not
this shriek that he squeezes from her lips
while her silent song overflows.

That Little Red Dress

She only meant to borrow it, slipped
the dress on in the shadow tent
of mannequins shouldering
muffled coats.

But the fabric fitted so well
– for a while at least –
clung like her skin, sagged
even less. It had to be owned.

And so she grew to fill it better:
changed the way she walked,
how she talked, the tilt
of her head, her hips, her heart until

she felt its satin touch
meld to her bones; red threads flowed
seamless into her blood –
labelled her tongue acrylic.

Russian Doll

She always liked organising:
Christmas, birthdays, the children's toys.

He used to sit and watch, admiring
the way she never forgot a thing.

All neatly packed up
and labelled in indelible ink.
For a rainy day, she used to say.

He didn't expect her brain
to file her memories into drawers
then throw away the keys.

The top drawer was the first to go:
the one where she stored yesterday's walk in the park
and the cardigan he bought for her birthday that week.

Then other things began to slip away:
their grandson's birth, that holiday to Greece.
Their wedding day.

Doctors say the bottom drawer will be the last to go:
the one where she is again a little girl;
his face a stranger's in her house,

where he sits and watches time remove
layer after layer of Russian dolls.

Eulogy

Dandelion, Löwenzahn, pissenlit
(the French name is so apt),
Taraxacum officinale...she once knew
the proper sound of most garden flowers.

Her love of language stemmed from Latin
lessons learned aloud at school.
When she was still ginger-haired, energetic,
she would coax her hollow seeds into poems
from which memories could grow;
sharp as lions' teeth.

Now her brain is a dandelion clock.
Each hour dispatches more spores.
No one knows where this grey matter goes;
dispersed, disposed.
The wind blows it like ashes.

Cutting up the Clock

I

Afterwards, we try to paste time back together,
snag our fingers on its hacked edges,
wonder why a bread knife
instead of neat scalpel.

We never get the numbers quite right.
Too much glue stops
the clock's cracked hands at seven.
Not even the hour we lost you.

Its heartbeat never sounds the same again:
tick-tock, tick-tick-tock...

II

The hour the clock stops does not mark
the moment you left
or even when absence sinks in.
It's just one arbitrary point in the minutes
that follow minutes.

Each morning, each evening
one of us must reach up, stretch
free the hand, unhook the stuck tock;
bump time out of its flatline.

III

Perhaps it wasn't a bread knife
but alcohol that stopped the clock,
unwound old-fashioned cogs,
disconnected watch batteries.

The glass of the wine bottle blurs
memories, distorts the ache
of missing you;
turns it mottled green.

IV

Suddenly there are couples everywhere –
kissing, talking, touching
eyes across the daytime dusk of the bar;
their clocks and watches not lost or broken
but abandoned knowingly.

I was once told (though I don't know why)
that to glass someone, the arm
must move upwards from jagged smash of fangs
to smooth neck in one fast arc.
But sometimes the bottle's glossed lip
bites as sharply.

V

There is another world where time
cogs backwards: tock-tick, tock-tick...
Echoes become voices, cold
pillows warm with your breath
and death is our start.

Cherry trees' bare branches
sweep confetti back into the sky
before shrinking down again
to buds, bulges, more bare branches.

A circle remains a circle and turning backwards
doesn't change what happens:
closed windows, echoing houses...
But at least in this world,
we're all forewarned.

VI

To come back from the dead is one thing,
to repeat it twelve-hourly is a different feat.

And still time's stitches won't dissolve.

We find ourselves nursing the hours
around resuscitation –
twice daily, like clockwork.

But routine heals.
As regularly as some walk dogs,
we leash and unleash our loss; keep it exercised.

VII

We've considered replacements;
choosing a new clock.

Then we see the dial's cracks
frown at us, reproach our lack of care.

But one day we miss the due pills, forget,
do not hear the tock stop.

When we notice, finally, the stillness of hands,
time has taken on its own rhythm:

nervous twitch replaced by feet itching to jig:
tick-tock, tick-tock, tickety-tock-tick.

Unframing the 'Skull with Yellow Roses'

I wanted a snake nesting in petals:
open-mouthed, hungry. Hissing.
But it reminded me of Blake's crimson bed,
bruised yellow.
    So I settled for bone munching on sun.
It says something, though I don't know what.
Maybe its yell is clenched on the 'ow'
of beauty's sting in the tail,
which I won't call hidden thorns – only a warning
that we choke on life as much as death.

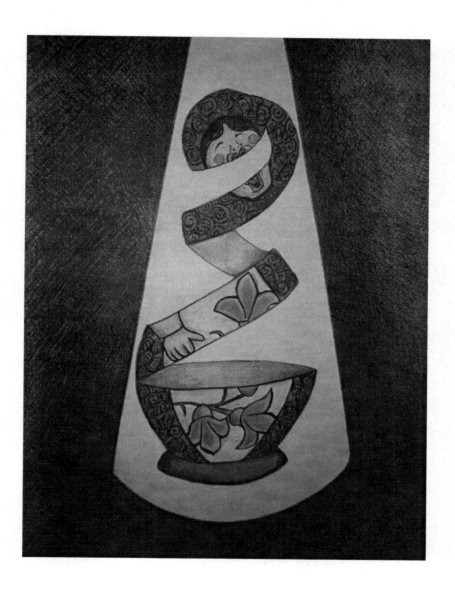

Circaidy Gregory

Independent Books for Independent Readers

Circaidy Gregory Press offers rewarding, unusual finds to readers who have high standards and enjoy searching out something just that little bit different. The list is mostly drawn from the work of authors we have met through Earlyworks Press competitions and club activities. Whilst Earlyworks Press exists to offer resources and good company to writers developing their careers, Circaidy Gregory is dedicated to the production of high quality, single author collections by writers we feel are going to appear in mainstream catalogues before too long.

Circaidy Gregory has produced four authors' first collections: 'Light in the Shade' – short stories by Pam Eaves, who came to our attention after being shortlisted several times in Earlyworks Press fiction competitions; 'wormwood, earth and honey' – poems by Catherine Edmunds who was shortlisted in the Earlyworks Press High Fantasy Challenge, sci-fi and poetry competitions; 'red silk slippers', Marilyn Francis's first poetry collection and Kay Green's own 'Jung's People' which was originally published by Andrew Hook's award-winning Elastic Press. Also on our lists are three novels, 'Crazy Bear', a dark comedy by Mark Rickman, a finalist in our 'Gender Genre' Challenge, 'Small Poisons', a magic realism novel by Catherine Edmunds and 'Charity's Child' – an unputdownable novel by Rosalie Warren, who was shortlisted in the Science Fiction Challenge and whose story 'Touching the Rabbit' caused a stir in the 'Gender Genre' Challenge. 'Charity's Child' has proved a great success with library reading groups and Rosalie has since gone on to secure a contract with a larger publisher.

To find out more about our authors, and our plans for the future, please visit our website – www.circaidygregory.co.uk

Kay Green, December 2009

www.circaidygregory.co.uk

red silk slippers

poems by Marilyn Francis

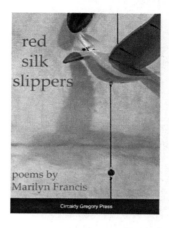

Marilyn Francis weaves magic. In this, her first poetry collection, she dodges Manchester's serious umbrellas, goes shopping for red rubber gloves, a green ball, pomegranates and a fish. She transports the reader into a world of shared memories and art galleries where the familiar is seen from an oblique angle. Turning the mirror on herself, she dissects the mole-like poet's task with a wry smile and slips into a world where a fly is caught in the drip of a clock.

'It's only a pack of cards,' says Alice, but all is not what it seems in this White Rabbit world of dreams.

Turn the pages and two old birds in owlish specs peep back from the depths of the floral chintz, a man fries an egg in the road somewhere off Oxford Street, and cows big as wardrobes dare you to cross.

As surreal as a de Chirico creation perhaps, but this is an accessible, welcoming book of real-world poems - as real as those red silk slippers from Thailand.

ISBN 978-1-906451-13-4

£6.50 + £1 p&p to UK Addresses

order from your local independent bookshop or buy online at

www.circaidygregory.co.uk

wormwood, earth and honey

selected poems by Catherine Edmunds

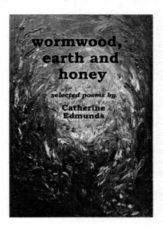

This, her first poetry collection, is accessible but never trivial: warm, earthy, intelligent and – just when you begin to snuggle into the intimacy of it – spiked with fire and venom.

Read, relish, enjoy.   - Wendy Robertson, novelist

This is poetry for a rainy day; to cheer you with colour, make you realise 'clouds dropped lumps of water' on everybody at some time, or giggle at the wry humour.

                                                - Pam Eaves, author

I give this book my Supreme Golden Syrup Pudding Award...
I read it twice before lunch, and now I'm off back for thirds.

                                 - John Irvine, poet and editor

ISBN 978-1-906451-04-2
£6.50 + £1 p&p to UK Addresses
order from your local independent bookshop or buy online at

www.circaidygregory.co.uk